CONTENTS

Plants and animals..............4

Animal diets 6

Predators and prey 8

What is a food chain? 10

Seashore food chains 12

Woodland food chains........ 14

Ocean food chains 16

Rainforest food chains....... 18

Humans........................ 20

Quiz 22

Glossary....................... 23

Index.......................... 24

Answers........................ 24

PLANTS AND ANIMALS

Plants and animals are living things. This means that they move, grow and, one day, will die. All living things need food and water to **survive**.

Plants, such as this oak tree, make their own food in their leaves using sunlight, air and water.

FACT CAT

Izzi Howell

WAYLAND
www.waylandbooks.co.uk

FACT CAT

Get your paws on this fantastic new mega-series from Wayland!

Join our Fact Cat on a journey of fun learning about every subject under the sun!

Published in Great Britain in 2018 by Wayland
Copyright © Wayland 2016

All rights reserved
ISBN: 978 1 5263 0536 7
10 9 8 7 6 5 4 3 2 1

Wayland
An imprint of Hachette Children's Group
Part of Hodder & Stoughton
Carmelite House
50 Victoria Embankment
London EC4Y 0DZ

An Hachette UK Company
www.hachette.co.uk
www.hachettechildrens.co.uk

A catalogue for this title is available from
the British Library
Printed and bound in China

Produced for Wayland by
White-Thomson Publishing Ltd
www.wtpub.co.uk

Editor: Izzi Howell
Design: Clare Nicholas
Fact Cat illustrations: Shutterstock/Julien Troneur
Other illustrations: Stefan Chabluk
Consultant: Karina Philip

Picture and illustration credits:
iStock: Kerstin Waurick 4, Jamie_Hall 10r, Kenneth Canning 13r, cdascher 17r; Shutterstock: Gleb Tarro cover, Mark Medcalf title page and 9, Paul S. Wolf 5, mark Higgins 6, Andrey Pavlov 7l, Sergey Uryadnikov 7r, Cathy Keifer 8, Inga Dudkina 10l, 12l, 13l and 17l, Erni 10c, Lynn Watson 11l, Villiers Steyn 11c, Johan Swanepoel 11r, Eskemar 12c, Doin Oakenhelm 12r, Zharate 13c, Darlene Hewson 14, gubernat 15l, Lisa S 15c, Bo Valentino 15r, Longjourneys16, John A. Anderson 17c, milosk50 18, Pedro Josa Marques Veiga Libario 19l, Vilainecrevette 19c, worldswildlifewonders 19r, Maks Narodenko 20, irin-k 21t, Tom Bird 21c, Samuel Borges Photography 21b.
Every effort has been made to clear copyright.
Should there be any inadvertent omission,
please apply to the publisher for rectification.

The author, Izzi Howell, is a writer and editor specialising in children's educational publishing.

The consultant, Karina Philip, is a teacher and a primary literacy consultant with an MA in creative writing.

FACT CAT FACT

There is a question for you to answer on each spread in this book. You can check your answers on page 24.

Toucans can peel fruit
with their beaks!

Unlike plants, animals can't make
their own food. They have to eat
other living things to survive. In
every **habitat**, there are different
foods for animals to eat.

Toucans eat fruit, such
as guavas, that grows on
trees in their rainforest
habitat. Find out the
names of two other foods
that toucans eat.

ANIMAL DIETS

There are three different types of animal diet: **herbivore, carnivore** and **omnivore**. Herbivores are animals that only eat plants. Horses and rabbits are examples of herbivores.

Koalas are herbivores. They mainly eat leaves from eucalyptus trees. In which country do koalas live?

Animals that eat other animals for food are called carnivores. Crocodiles and lions are examples of carnivores. Omnivores, such as bears and blackbirds, eat plants and animals.

The crocodile uses its tail to jump up to catch **prey**.

Ants are omnivores. They eat other insects and fruit.

FACT CAT **FACT**

When crocodiles catch a large prey animal, they eat so much of it that they don't need to eat again for a week. Crocodiles only eat around 50 times a year!

PREDATORS AND PREY

Most carnivores and omnivores are **predators**. Predators are animals that kill other animals for food. Herbivores are usually prey. This means that other animals eat them for food.

Praying mantises kill and eat butterflies. Which animal is the predator and which is the prey?

Birds of prey, such as this osprey, use their claws to catch fish from lakes and rivers.

Some predators, such as tigers, have big teeth and **claws** to help them catch prey. To keep safe, some types of prey have good eyesight and hearing so that they can tell when a predator is nearby.

FACT CAT FACT

Some carnivores and omnivores eat animals that are already dead. Animals that do this are called **scavengers**.

WHAT IS A FOOD CHAIN?

Food chains are a way of showing how living things depend on each other for food. Food chains are made up of animals and plants. They are different in every habitat.

We can use a food chain to show that kingfishers eat minnows in river habitats.

algae (al-gee)

minnow

eaten by

kingfisher

eaten by

grass

zebra

eaten by

lion

eaten by

This is a food chain from the **savannahs** of Africa. Zebras eat grass and lions eat zebras. Which animal is a herbivore in this food chain?

Plants are at the beginning of every food chain. Plants are followed by the herbivores that eat the plants. At the end, there are the omnivores or carnivores that eat the herbivores.

Female lions catch most of the food for their pride (lions that live together in a group).

SEASHORE FOOD CHAINS

algae

herring

Birds such as puffins live on **cliffs** by the seashore. They fly down to the ocean to catch fish to eat.

puffin

eaten by

eaten by

A seashore is an area of land next to an ocean. Some plants and animals live away from the water on the sand or rocks. Other animals live in the water, close to the shore.

algae

limpet

starfish

eaten by

eaten by

Rock pools are pools of seawater on the seashore. Small animals often live underwater in rock pools. They eat the shellfish and algae that live on the rocks.

Starfish can move out of rock pools to catch food such as limpets. Where is a starfish's mouth?

FACT CAT FACT

Limpets use their strong teeth to cut algae off rocks.

WOODLAND FOOD CHAINS

Woodlands are home to many types of animal, including large **mammals**, birds and tiny insects. It can be hard to spot insects because they live in logs and under fallen leaves.

Red foxes are woodland mammals. Foxes are omnivores – what kinds of plants and animals do they eat?

There is plenty of food for herbivores in woodland habitats. Herbivores, such as deer, eat the leaves and fruit of small plants and trees. Woodland carnivores, such as wolves, eat the herbivores.

In woodlands, common toads hunt and eat slugs.

daisy

slug

common toad

eaten by

eaten by

FACT CAT **FACT**

Common toads can live for up to 40 years!

OCEAN FOOD CHAINS

Most of the Earth's **surface** is covered by oceans. Fish, shellfish and ocean mammals spend all of their lives underwater. Plants such as seaweed and algae grow on the ocean floor.

Adult green sea turtles are herbivores. They eat sea grasses and algae.

FACT CAT FACT

Plants on the ocean floor can still make food from sunlight because the light travels down through the water.

Many predators, such as large fish and sharks, live in the ocean. These predators eat smaller fish that feed on algae.

algae

surgeonfish

reef shark

eaten by

eaten by

Reef sharks and surgeonfish live on coral reefs. Are reef sharks carnivores, herbivores or omnivores?

RAINFOREST FOOD CHAINS

Jaguars hunt for prey on the forest floor in the rainforests of South America.

In rainforests, many tall trees grow up from the forest floor. Most large animals live close to the ground, as they are too heavy to climb up into the trees.

mango

capuchin monkey

The harpy eagle is one of the biggest and most powerful birds of prey. Find out the name of another type of bird of prey.

eaten by

harpy eagle

Small birds and monkeys often live high in the branches of rainforest trees. They eat the fruit and leaves of rainforest plants.

eaten by

FACT CAT FACT

Harpy eagles can carry prey that is almost the same weight as they are!

HUMANS

Humans are also part of food chains because all of our food comes from plants and animals. Humans are usually at the end of the food chain.

Humans grow most of the plants that they eat, such as corn.

Humans grow plants and **raise** animals on farms. On a farm, a farmer grows grass for sheep to eat. Then, some humans eat meat from the sheep.

grass

sheep

eaten by

eaten by

human

FACT CAT FACT

You can drink sheep's milk and make cheese from it. What soft material do we also get from sheep?

Many farm animals, such as sheep, cows and goats, eat grass.

QUIZ Try to answer the questions below. Look back through the book to help you. Check your answers on page 24.

1 Plants aren't living things. True or not true?

a) true

b) not true

2 What is the name for an animal that only eats other animals?

a) herbivore

b) omnivore

c) carnivore

3 Tigers are predators. True or not true?

a) true

b) not true

4 What comes at the beginning of a food chain?

a) herbivores

b) plants

c) carnivores

5 Which of these plants grows in the ocean?

a) seaweed

b) oak tree

c) daisy

6 Humans grow most of the plants that they eat. True or not true?

a) true

b) not true

GLOSSARY

algae a plant-like living thing without a stem or leaves

bird of prey a large bird that kills smaller animals for food

carnivore an animal that only eats meat

claw a sharp curved nail on the foot of an animal

cliff high, steep rocks next to the ocean

coral reef a tropical sea habitat made from coral (a hard material made by a very small sea animal)

female describes an animal that can give birth to young or lay eggs from which young will hatch

food chain a way of showing how living things depend on each other for food

habitat the area where a plant or animal lives

herbivore an animal that only eats plants

mammal a type of animal with fur that gives birth to live young

omnivore an animal that eats plants and meat. 'Omni' means all.

predator an animal that kills and eats other animals

prey an animal that is killed and eaten by other animals

raise to look after an animal or plant as it grows

rock pool a pool of seawater on a rocky beach

savannah a flat area of land covered in grass and some trees

scavenger an animal that feeds on the bodies of other dead animals

surface the top part of something

survive to stay alive and not die

INDEX

algae 10, 12, 13, 16, 17

carnivores 6, 7, 8, 9, 11, 15

farms 20, 21

herbivores 6, 8, 11, 15, 16

humans 20–21

leaves 4, 6, 14, 15, 19

living things 4, 5, 10

oceans 12, 13, 16–17,

omnivores 6, 7, 8, 9, 11, 14

predators 8–9, 17

prey 7, 8–9, 18, 19

rainforests 5, 18–19

rivers 9, 10

rock pools 13

savannahs 11

scavengers 9

seashore 12–13

sunlight 4, 16

trees 4, 5, 6, 15, 18, 19

woodlands 14–15

ANSWERS

Pages 4–21

Page 5: Some foods include insects, the eggs of other animals and lizards.

Page 6: Australia

Page 8: The praying mantis is the predator and the butterfly is the prey.

Page 11: The zebra

Page 13: In the centre of the underneath of its body.

Page 14: Some foods include rabbits, birds, fruit, fish and worms.

Page 17: Carnivores

Page 19: Some birds of prey include hawks and falcons.

Page 21: Wool

Quiz answers

1 not true – plants and animals are living things.

2 c - carnivore

3 true

4 b - plants

5 a - seaweed

6 true